DISCOVER
Rain Forests

Contributing Writer
Lynne Hardie Baptista

Consultant
Richard Block

Publications International, Ltd.

Louis Weber, C.E.O.
Publications International, Ltd.
7373 North Cicero Avenue
Lincolnwood, IL 60646

Manufactured in U.S.A.

8 7 6 5 4 3 2 1

ISBN 1-56173-426-8

Photo Credits:

Front cover: **Animals Animals:** Klaus Uhlenhut (center); Raymond A. Mendez (top); **Siede/Preis Photography** (bottom).

Back cover: **Tom & Michele Grimm/International Stock Photography:** (bottom); D. **Marklin/FPG International**: (top).

Thomas C. Boyden: 34 (left & right); **Bruce Coleman, Inc.:** 15 (bottom right), 24 (center), 26 (bottom left); James H. Carmichael: 31 (right center), 32 (top left); J.S.G. Grande: (bottom left); Kjell B. Sandved: 35 (bottom left); Sullivan & Rogers: 32 (top right); **FPG International:** 6 (center), 43 (top left), back end sheet (top left); Barbara Adams: 22 (bottom); Laurance B. Aluppy: 9 (center); T. Alvez: Front end sheet (top right); M. Bruce: 30 (bottom); Charles Fitch: Contents (right center), 16 (top left); Robert Graham: 30 (top); Farrell Grehan: 18 (top); M.P. Kahl: 19 (top left); Peter B. Kaplan: 43 (right center); Lee Kuhn: 18 (bottom left), 19 (top center); Guy Marche: 38 (top right); Suzanne Murphy: Front end sheet (top left); Jeffry W. Myers: 38 (bottom right); Leonard Lee Rue III: 19 (bottom); A. Schmidecker: 11 (top & bottom); Jerry Sieve: 42 (center); Eric Silberg: 9 (top); Latin Stock: Contents (bottom left); Jeffery Sylvester: 28 (top), 42 (bottom); The Telegraph Colour Library: Front end sheet (center); Nikolay Zurek: 38 (bottom left); **Steven Holt:** Contents (bottom right), 17 (top), 32 (bottom right); **International Stock Photography:** George Ancona: 10 (bottom left); Chad Ehlers: 6 (top), 10 (top); Frank Grant: 30 (center); Henry Mills: Back end sheet (bottom right); Stephen S. Myers: 35 (center); Peter Symasko: 12 (top); Peter Walton: 8 (left); **Lou Jost:** 31 (top & bottom), 34 (bottom); **Zig Leszczynski:** Contents (left center), 6 (bottom), 10 (bottom right), 16 (bottom left), 17 (bottom), 21, 25 (top), 26 (top right), 28 (center); **Scott Lewis:** 4 (center & bottom), 15 (top), 36 (top), 40 (top), 41 (bottom); **Luiz C. Marigo/Peter Arnold, Inc.:** 35 (top); **Rainbow:** Michael J. Doolittle: Front end sheet (right center), 20 (center & bottom), 27 (top left & top right), 28 (bottom), 37, 40 (bottom), back end sheet (bottom left); Dean Hulse: 12 (bottom); Steve Lissay: 13; Dan McCoy: 26 (bottom right), 42 (top); **Kevin Schafer:** Contents (top), 1, 18 (bottom right), 22 (top), 23 (center), 26 (top left), 31 (left center); **Kevin Schafer & Martha Hill:** Front end sheet (bottom), 4 (top), 5, 7 (bottom), 8 (right), 9 (bottom), 12 (center), 15 (bottom left), 20 (top), 23 (top), 24 (bottom), 25 (bottom left & bottom right), 27 (bottom left & right), 29, 33 (center), 38 (top left), 39 (top left & top right), 43 (top right & bottom); **Tom Stack & Associates:** Nancy Adams: 22 (center); Mary Clay: 11 (left); David M. Dennis: 33 (bottom); Chip & Jill Isenhart: Back end sheet (center); Brian Parker: Back end sheet (top right); Richard P. Smith: 24 (top); Jack Swenson: 8 (top); **Robin White/FotoLex Associates:** 7 (top & center), 14, 16 (top right & bottom right), 17 (center), 19 (top right), 23 (bottom), 33 (top), 35 (bottom right), 36 (bottom), 39 (bottom), 40 (center), 41 (top & center).

Illustrations: Pablo Montes O'Neill.

Lynne Hardie Baptista is the author of numerous articles and award-winning education programs on wildlife conservation and the environment. She is the public information and education specialist of the World Wildlife Fund and is now manager of the education project "Windows on the Wild."

Richard Block has been the director of public programs at the World Wildlife Fund since 1987. He has previously been curator of education at Zoo Atlanta and a lecturer at the School of Natural Resources, the University of Michigan. His degrees are in environmental studies and natural resources.

CONTENTS

WELCOME TO THE RAIN FOREST.

Colorful, screeching birds. Slow, deliberate sloths. Lizards that fly, and insects that look like plants. Wonderful, wet, and wild! Rain forests are the richest places on earth. They are rich not with diamonds or gold, but with  life. Rain forests cover just six percent of Earth's surface, but they are home to more than half the species of plants and animals in the world.

Rain forests are full of mystery and promise. We have much to learn from them and about them. Scientists  have really just started to unlock the secrets that wait there for discovery. At the same time, we are destroying rain forests at an alarming rate.

4

Some rain forests that are still alive today have changed very little for millions of years.

The terms *jungle* and *rain forest* are actually interchangeable; they mean the same thing.

Tigers and boa constrictors are two of the rain forest inhabitants that people have always feared.

What do you think when you hear the term *rain forest?* Lions and tigers. Weird insects. Huge man-eating snakes. Giant hairy spiders. Headhunters and cannibals. Hot and steamy. Dark and forbidding. Tangled, twisted vines. An endless dark forest. A jungle!

Such images are common in a jungle story, but they don't describe a real rain forest very well. You can easily walk through the floor of the rain forest. Although the plant life is lush, most of the tangled leaves and vines grow in the upper layers. Also, some native tribes may be unfriendly or even hostile to outsiders, but most of them are peaceful and generous. The rain forest does hold many potentially dangerous animals, but as a rule they try to avoid the commotion caused by noisy visitors like us.

The first people to explore rain forests came for the great wealth they could find. Most of these adventurers braved the unknown new world in search of jewels, gold, slaves, and lost civilizations.

Today, the rain forest attracts people like a magnet. People continue to go there to seek the riches within the rain forest. Scientists go there to study the plants, animals, and people. They have only just begun to unlock the natural wonders of the rain forest. Maybe someday you will go there, too!

Tropical rain forests are lush, green regions that circle Earth. They are hot and humid all year round. The thing that probably tells you the most about rain forests, though, is that there is no one kind. There are actually about 40 different types of rain forests. Some receive more rain than others, and we call them *wet* rain forests. Some rain forests grow in mountainous areas, and we call them *montane* (mahn-TAYN) rain forests. There are even *dry* rain forests that get less rain than other rain forest regions. Different rain forests have different kinds of soils.

Still, rain forests share some basic features. Rain forests are very old. Scientists believe that the rain forest environment may be the oldest type of habitat in the world. Dinosaurs lived in habitats very similar to today's rain forests.

At one time, rain forest regions stretched northward into what is now the United States. They once formed a solid green belt around the middle of Earth near the Equator. They covered over four billion acres—about 20 percent of Earth's total land surface. For millions of years, rain forests grew and shrank as the worldwide climate changed, but they never disappeared.

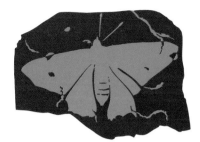

Scientists have even found fossils of rain forest plants and animals from more than 45 million years ago!

Dry rain forests (above and right) are home to many plant and animal species. Many montane rain forests (below) are always covered in a thick, cloudy mist.

WELCOME TO THE RAIN FOREST

Some very wet rain forests can get more than 400 inches of rain each year!

True to their name, rain forests receive an incredible amount of rain. About 60 inches of rain falls every year in an average rain forest. Temperatures usually range between 70° and 85°F, but it can get much warmer. The temperature at night rarely drops below 70°F.

The constant moist and warm conditions in the rain forest allow an astounding variety of plants and animals to thrive. On a single acre of rain forest, you may find about ten times as many tree species as in a forest in a temperate region.

Most of the plants and animals that live in the rain forest live nowhere else in the world. Scientists are not even sure how many plants and animals live in the world's rain forests because not all rain forest areas have been studied. There are probably between five million and 30 million rain forest species that we have not discovered yet! Most of these species are probably insects and other *invertebrates*, or animals that have no backbones.

In temperate areas like Europe and North America, changes in temperature mark the coming and going of the seasons. In the tropics, rainfall defines the seasons. Most tropical areas have one dry season and one wet season.

Rain forests are sometimes called green treasure chests because they are so rich with life. People might think that rain forests are very tough and strong because they support so many living creatures. In fact, the opposite is true. The rain forest is a very fragile place. Beneath the thick green layer of trees and shrubs, the soil that supports the rain forest is thin and poor in nutrients. In all forests, water washes away some of the nutrients in the top layer of the soil every time it rains. In the rain forest, it can rain very hard every day.

Most of the nutrients and energy in the rain forest are not free to be taken from the soil. Instead, they are locked up in living plants and animals. When a creature dies or a leaf falls, bacteria, fungi, and tiny invertebrates quickly go to work to break it down. They decompose the debris into nutrients, some of which they use and some of which go into the soil. The plants' roots must absorb these nutrients before the rain can wash them away. This natural process must happen very quickly, or the valuable nutrients will be lost. The cycle of life and death in the rain forest is very fast and very efficient. In the rain forest, nothing is wasted and everything is recycled.

The rainfall has been washing nutrients out of the soil for thousands of years. The rain forest soil has a very thin top layer with few nutrients. Most rain forest plants have very thin roots that grow only in this top layer.

Nutrients return to the soil when a plant or animal dies or when a leaf or a piece of fruit falls to the forest floor. Mushrooms and other decomposers make this system possible.

The world has three major regions of tropical rain forests: the Amazon basin of South America, Africa's Congo basin, and the Malay archipelago (ar-kuh-PEL-uh-go) in the South Pacific.

South America has the largest rain forest in the world. This region is known as the Amazon basin or Amazonia, named for the mighty Amazon River. Most of the Amazonian rain forest is in Brazil, but large portions also grow in neighboring Peru, Colombia, and Ecuador.

Rain forests also grow in the Caribbean. In Central America, rain forests still grow in Guatemala, Honduras, Nicaragua, Belize, Costa Rica, and Panama.

South American rain forests are home to their own unique animal species. If you are lucky, you might see a slow-moving sloth or a quick, silent jaguar. They each travel through the trees in their own unique way. You might spy a colorful toucan as it gobbles fruit with its huge bill or a tiny hummingbird as it moves from flower to flower and sips nectar.

This acrobatic spider monkey will spend its life among the treetops of the Colombian rain forest.

The anteater is one of the Amazon's strange-looking creatures.

In Africa, rain forests occur in two main blocks—one along the south coast of West Africa and one centered in the country of Zaire. Businesses probably value the African rain forests most for the beautiful species of hardwood trees that grow there. Loggers have cut down countless mahogany and ebony trees. These trees are now very rare.

Interesting animals are also native to Africa's rain forests. The okapi (o-KAHP-ee) was first discovered by

Elephants strip leaves and bark from the trees of the West African rain forest.

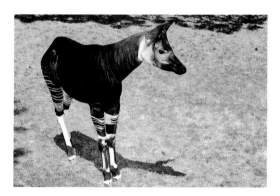

scientists in 1900. The endangered mountain gorilla and the forest elephant are two of the largest residents of the African rain forest.

The rain forests in Southeast Asia and Australia do not grow in huge areas like they do in South America and Africa. Instead, they are spread out mostly over the many island countries in that region.

Rain forests in Asia are home to Asian elephants, tigers, and orangutans—all endangered species. Rain forests in Asia are also home to some of the most valuable tree species in the world.

The rain forests in Asia are disappearing the fastest. Inhabitants such as the orangutan are disappearing along with them.

11

RAIN FORESTS HAVE LAYERS,

but they are not very easy to see. If you were lucky enough to fly over a rain forest in an airplane, you would see what looks like a solid carpet of green. But what is beneath this magnificent carpet?

All forests have layers. In fact, all plant communities have layers. Even your front lawn has two layers—the grass grows above a lower layer of moss. The trees, shrubs, vines, ferns, and other plants that grow in rain forests make up a much more complex system. Scientists divide rain forests into four basic layers—the emergent layer, the canopy, the understory, and the forest floor.

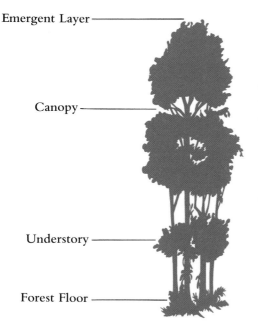

Emergent Layer

Canopy

Understory

Forest Floor

Even with its layers, the rain forest is still one connected system from top to bottom.

At first glance, a rain forest will look like a solid green wall from top to bottom. The boundaries between  layers are not clear, and no two sections of rain forest will be the same.

In order to divide a rain forest into layers, scientists start with a small patch. They clear the area of vines and shrubs. Next, they measure the position and height of each plant and identify it by species. They plot this information on a chart as a sample of how plants grow in that area of rain forest. They can then compare and contrast samples from different patches in one rain forest or from patches in different rain forests.

Conditions change from one layer to the next, so the species that live in each layer change too. Each layer provides a special habitat for a wealth of different species. Every layer also has special challenges for survival. Every plant or animal needs special features that will allow it to survive in the layer that serves as its home.

The different layers also have an effect on each other. The top of the forest controls how much light and water reach the lower layers. On the forest floor, insects and other decomposers recycle the nutrients that creatures in the upper layers need to survive.

The layers of a rain forest allow more species to find homes there. Sometimes a single acre of rain forest will have more than 350 different plant species growing on it.

14

The rain forest usually supports one or two giant trees per acre that tower above all the other plants. The tops of these *emergents* sprout above the dense jungle like huge umbrellas. Emergents are often about 115 to 150 feet tall, but some can reach up to 250 feet, as high as a 25 story building!

Because emergent trees are the tallest, they have a different environment than the rest of the rain forest. These trees get the first share of the strong sunshine that beats down on the equator. They must survive hot and changing temperatures, low humidity, and strong winds.

Many giant trees have unusual root structures. Some species have thick, ridged *buttress roots* that give extra support. These buttresses grow above ground and surround the tree. Buttresses may reach 30 feet up the trunk of the tree and spread even further along the ground.

Animals visit the emergent layer to munch on the leaves, fruits, and seeds that grow there, to escape predators, or even just to sunbathe! Woodpeckers, hawks, and eagles visit the emergent layer frequently. High-flying butterflies also are common.

The emergent trees usually have long, slender branches.

Buttress roots help to keep the tree standing when large gusts of wind pass overhead, and they support the tree in the shallow rain forest soil. The roots may also help by spreading the great weight of the tree over a larger area of ground.

The emergents are the oldest trees in the rain forest, but it is hard to tell their exact ages.

Africa's colobus (KAHL-uh-bas) monkey will sometimes visit the emergent layer to munch on leaves and take a break from its constant watch for predators.

15

Some trees in the canopy have *stilt roots*. Stilt roots are long and thin. They surround the base of a tree trunk in the form of a triangle. Like buttress roots, they provide extra support.

Orchids are probably the best-known epiphytes. There are around 20,000 species of them.

Bromeliads come in many different shapes and colors. Sometimes the little pool that forms in the bromeliad will become a small habitat all of its own. Tiny frogs, salamanders, aquatic plants, and insects find the little pools to be safe, secure places to live and breed.

Beneath the swaying tops of the giant emergents grows a second thick layer of shorter trees. The tops of these trees overlap into what looks like a solid green roof. This is the *canopy* layer.

The trees that form the canopy are usually between 65 and 100 feet tall. Many are still growing, and eventually they may join the emergent layer. Other species will never grow past the canopy no matter how long they live.

Other plants share the canopy layer with these tall trees. *Epiphytes* (E-puh-fytz) are plants that are totally dependent on other plants for support. They attach themselves to a tree or other plant and let their roots drape downward. They get their nourishment from dead leaves and animals that fall from above, get caught in their roots, and decay.

Another group of plants that grows in the canopy is the *bromeliads* (bro-MEE-lee-adz). Bromeliads are another kind of epiphyte, and they are related to the pineapple. Because they have no roots growing in the ground, bromeliads must soak up water and nutrients in another way. Some bromeliads have what look like small cups surrounded by leaves. The cups catch rainwater and falling bits of plants, insects, and other forest litter.

Vines, some of which are called *lianas* (lee-AH-nuhz), grow on the trees in the canopy, too. The dense leaves and branches of the trees overlap with the vines, epiphytes, ferns, and other plants to form a thick roof. This umbrella that tops the canopy limits the amount of sunlight and rain that reaches the forest floor.

Many of the large animals that live in the rain forest make their homes in the canopy. Some spend almost all of their lives there. They hunt, eat, sleep, and even give birth to their babies high in the trees!

Some animals have evolved ways to glide from tree to tree or from the canopy to lower levels in the rain forest. This allows them to escape predators and to search for food over a larger area of the rain forest. Flying squirrels have thick folds of skin that stretch along their bodies from their wrists to their ankles. Wallace's flying frog is the only frog that can glide. It has skin flaps between each toe that open like small parachutes when the frog jumps. These frogs can glide up to 40 feet! Parachute geckos have skin flaps on either side of their heads and along their bodies. They can also sail from tree to tree. Sloths, orangutans, and parrots also make their homes in the canopy.

Some vines begin life at the forest floor, slowly creeping up through the trees. Others start as seeds in the treetops and drop their roots to the ground.

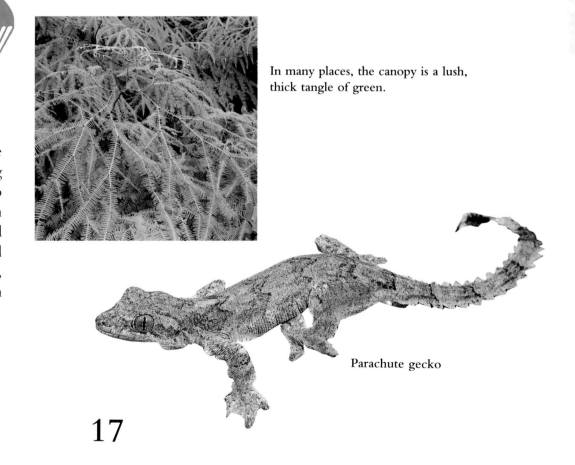

In many places, the canopy is a lush, thick tangle of green.

Parachute gecko

17

Many plants that grow in this layer are young trees that will eventually grow high into the canopy layer. Other plants found here are shrubs, miniature trees, dwarf palms, and herbs.

Below the canopy are small trees and shrubs that usually will not grow higher than about 15 feet. The plants that live in the *understory* face a very difficult environment. The canopy layer overhead acts almost like a shield from the sun, the rain, and the wind. The understory is very dim and still. To survive, understory plants have adapted broad, thin, flat leaves that allow them to collect as much light as possible.

Many of the creatures in the understory have become *nocturnal* because they are often the prey of large cats, snakes, and birds. Nocturnal animals are active during the night and sleep during the day. Most nocturnal animals, such as the night monkey or the bizarre aye-aye (EYE-eye), have huge eyes and excellent night vision. Some bats use sound echoes to hunt and to avoid bumping into things in the darkness.

Only five percent of the rain forests' sunlight reaches the understory.

Ocelot

Coatimundi

Spotted cats such as the jaguar, the ocelot (AHS-uh-laht), and the clouded leopard also live in the understory. They spend much of their time hunting for deer, rodents, and birds. Other animals that spend much of their time in the understory are emerald tree boas, coatimundis, and lemurs.

18

It is a long way from the top of the tallest tree in the emergent layer to the forest floor—as much as 250 feet. On the forest floor it is very dark and the air is very quiet and still. The plant life growing in the three layers above keeps out almost all of the light, wind, and rain.

Still the forest floor is brimming with life. Along with fungi and lichens, millions of invertebrates—ants, termites, spiders, land crabs, earthworms, and beetles—live on or just below the surface of the forest floor. These are the decomposers that keep the forest clean by recycling debris into life-giving nutrients.

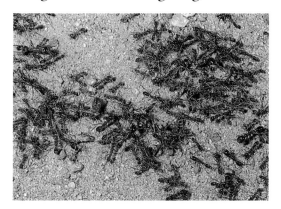

Some mammal species also live on the forest floor. Many of these are specially suited to root out the invertebrates that live just under the topsoil. The giant anteater has an incredibly long tongue and snout to suck out ants and termites from their nests. The white-lipped peccary (PEK-uh-ree) and the Malayan tapir (TAY-pur) use their broad snouts to root out insects and worms. Elephants and gorillas are also common visitors to the floor of the rain forest.

Lichens

Only a few large plants can grow under the harsh conditions of the forest floor—some seedlings, herbs, and ferns.

When one tree dies, many other plant species can begin to grow. They quickly take over the patch of rain forest soil along with its sunlight and water.

The peccary is one of the large animals that manages to live on the forest floor in South America.

19

EXOTIC LIFE FORMS

fill every corner of the rain forest. Imagine that you are a scientist and your job is to go to Brazil and count as many species of insects, birds, mammals, and plants as you can. You would be there for a long, long time. Thousands upon thousands of species live in just that one rain forest. And they are scattered from the top of the tallest trees to just beneath the forest floor.

The rain forest is bursting with life! More than half of Earth's plant and animal species make their homes there. Each one has adapted its own unique, sometimes strange ways of coping with rain forest life. Scientists say that there may be millions of species living in rain forests that no one has ever seen.

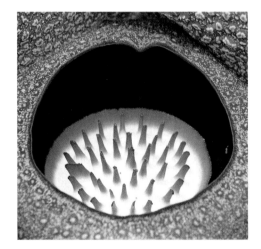

A sloth's hair grows toward its back so that rain drops will roll off as the animal hangs upside down. Algae grow on the hairs and give the sloth a muddy color that helps it blend in to the trees.

Sloths never move quickly. Their slow pace helps protect them from the keen eyes of predators. Sloths like to hang upside down from branches in the canopy layer, and they almost never go down to the forest floor.

The South American tamandua (tuh-MAN-doo-wuh) is a type of anteater that is very clumsy on the ground. With the help of its prehensile tail, it is very much at home high in the trees. The tamandua specializes in eating termites and ants and finds them with its keen sense of smell. The tamandua itself has a very bad odor, and it has earned the nickname "stinker of the forest."

The okapi is a very unusual hoofed animal that looks like it is half deer and half zebra. It is actually a relative of the giraffe. Scientists first discovered the okapi in 1900 deep in the rain forests of Zaire, a country in Africa. The okapi eats leaves that it strips from trees in the understory. The okapi's tongue is so long—14 inches—that it can even use it to clean its own eyes and ears!

The clouded leopard can run down trees headfirst, climb upside down, and swing by a single hind paw.

The clouded leopard is one of the top predators in the rain forest of Southeast Asia. This rare spotted cat gets its name from the soft edges it has to its large spots. It has no enemies except humans, who kill clouded leopards for their beautiful coats.

The tapir of Southeast Asia is a piglike mammal that uses its long, tapering snout to browse on grasses, leaves, and fruits. They are good swimmers and spend much of their time near water.

The capybara (cap-i-BAYR-uh) is a funny-looking mammal that just happens to be the world's largest rodent. This South American resident looks something like a giant guinea pig. Capybaras are usually three to four feet long. They eat grasses that grow in or near water. Some people consider capybara meat extremely tasty. In Venezuela, there are even capybara "ranches" where these giant rodents are raised like cattle!

Howler monkeys get their name from their very loud voices that roar through the rain forests of South America. Howlers live in groups of 20 or so monkeys and will defend their homes from other howler monkeys by shouting and shrieking at them. Their howls can be heard over half a mile away.

The golden lion tamarin (TAM-uh-ruhn) is a bright orange, squirrel-sized monkey that lives in only one small section of the Brazilian rain forest. The golden lion tamarin lives in family groups of two to nine monkeys and eats insects, small lizards, and fruits. Many golden lion tamarins have been captured for pets, and almost all of their rain forest home has been destroyed. The golden lion tamarin is an endangered species and is a symbol of wildlife conservation in Brazil.

Capybaras live in large groups near water. Folds of skin between their toes help make them excellent swimmers.

Howler monkeys spend most of their time in the canopy layer and very rarely come to the ground.

Many of these animals are in danger of becoming extinct.

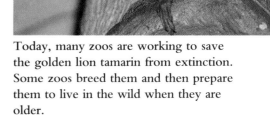

Today, many zoos are working to save the golden lion tamarin from extinction. Some zoos breed them and then prepare them to live in the wild when they are older.

The harpy eagle is the largest eagle in the world.

The harpy eagle is the top predator in the emergent layer of South America's rain forests. It can streak through the trees at speeds close to 50 miles per hour and then grasp its prey in its deadly sharp talons. The harpy eagle eats monkeys, sloths, opossums, and snakes.

The toucan (TOO-kan) is probably one of the most well-known birds of the rain forest. It spends much of its time in the emergent and canopy layers with as many as 12 others of its kind. The toucan's bill is much lighter than it looks, and the bird uses the tip to snip off small fruits and berries. The jagged edge of the bill helps the bird bite off larger pieces of fruit.

The bowerbird of Australia and Papua New Guinea uses the forest floor in a very unusual way. The male bowerbird builds an elaborate home, called a bower, out of grasses, leaves, and twigs. He will even decorate his bower with brightly-colored berries and feathers. He does all of this to attract a female bowerbird.

Woodpeckers fly through all levels of the forest in search of insects. Their strong bills work like a chisel to dig into tree bark. Their long, sticky, barbed tongues pull out burrowing bugs and larvae. As they pound into a tree, woodpeckers use their tails and long, sharp claws for support.

The male bowerbird is waiting outside while a female inspects his bower.

The toucan sometimes eats insects, spiders, and even small birds.

Poison-arrow frogs are brightly colored to warn predators that their skins are very poisonous. Indians in the Amazon rain forest use their poison to coat the tips of the arrows they use for hunting. Poison-arrow frogs live in the understory.

Chameleons (kuh-MEE-lee-uhnz) can lighten or darken their skin to blend in to their surroundings in the Asian and African rain forests. They are able to change color with special pigment cells in their skin. Chameleons can look at two things at once because their eyes can move in different directions at the same time! They have long, sticky tongues that can shoot out with great accuracy to snap up insects and spiders.

Freshwater crocodiles, or freshies, live in the rivers and streams that flow through the rain forest in Australia and Papua New Guinea. At night, they wait just beneath the surface of the water for a thirsty animal to come to the water's edge. The crocs knock their prey over with a swing of the tail and drag it underwater with their huge jaws.

The green tree python is a beautiful green snake that blends well with the leaves of the canopy. It is a very deadly predator that feeds on the birds, small mammals, and tree frogs of Southeast Asia. When the snake catches a victim, it wraps itself around the prey and squeezes until the victim suffocates.

The poison in this tiny frog is one of the strongest natural poisons in the world—one millionth of an ounce can kill a dog.

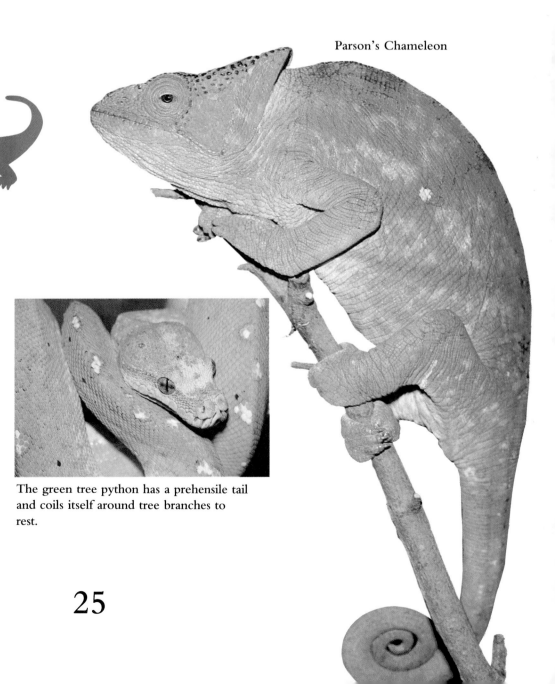

Parson's Chameleon

The green tree python has a prehensile tail and coils itself around tree branches to rest.

EXOTIC LIFE FORMS

One to two million leaf-cutter ants may live in one nest, called a colony. A large colony may need seven pounds of leaves per day to keep the fungus garden growing.

Although they look quite scary, bird-eating spiders are actually shy creatures and will only attack a human if they are attacked first. A bite from this spider is very painful but usually not fatal.

Birdwing butterfly

Leaf-cutter ants of Central and South America are the farmers of the insect world. They collect pieces of leaves and flowers and carry them to their underground nest. The ants chew up the bits of plant to create a pulpy material. The material provides food for a layer of fungus to grow. The ants then use that fungus for their own food.

Also known as tarantulas, bird-eating spiders are large enough to attack birds, reptiles, and small mammals. These spiders hunt at night in the South American rain forests. Some hide on the forest floor under leaves and stones, waiting for their prey to walk by. Others live and hunt in the trees. Their thick covering of hair is sensitive to movement and helps them detect their prey.

Birdwing butterflies of New Guinea are some of the largest and most beautiful butterflies in the world. Their wingspan can be as much as eight inches wide. Their brightly colored wings flash in the sun. Their colors are a signal to other animals that they are poisonous. Birdwing butterflies spend most of their time in the upper layers of the rain forest, but they will fly down to the forest floor to find food or to drink from a puddle. Because of their beauty, birdwing butterflies are in great demand by butterfly collectors and are becoming very rare.

Lianas (lee-AH-nuhz) are thick, ropelike vines that grow on trees for support. They begin life as seedlings on the forest floor and grow up the trunks of trees. Or, they attach themselves to a small tree and hitch a ride up into the canopy as the tree grows. Lianas do not twine around tree trunks but hang freely.

Strangler figs start life as seeds dropped by birds high on the branch of a tree. A seedling will send long roots down the trunk of the support tree to the forest floor. As the strangler fig grows, more roots are sent down and form a web around the trunk of the tree.

The rafflesia (ruh-FLEE-zhee-uh) plant has the broadest flower in the world—it can grow to three feet across. The rafflesia plant lives on the forest floor in Southeast Asia. It is a parasite that gets all of its energy from other plants and none from the sun. The huge rafflesia flower smells like rotting meat! This attracts certain insects that will pollinate the flowers.

Bird's nest ferns are epiphytes. They attach themselves to other plants but they do not steal nutrients from them. These ferns are found high in the canopy layer and have long leaves that grow in the shape of a cup. Water and falling plant matter from above fall into this cup and are held there. From this pool the bird's nest fern draws water and nutrients.

This bird's nest fern is growing on a tree trunk in the rain forest of Malaysia.

The rafflesia flower can grow to three feet across, and it smells like rotten meat!

Strangler figs can completely surround their host tree and block the sunlight it needs. The tree may die, but the fig will continue to grow.

27

STRUGGLING TO SURVIVE is an everyday part of life in the rain forest. Every animal must meet the same challenges. They compete with each other for food and water, they protect themselves from predators, and they raise their young. Plants living in the rain forest also face the same kinds of survival challenges.

Each species has its own unique, sometimes amazing ways to survive. When these adaptations work, the creatures pass them on to the next generation. When they don't work, the creatures die and the adaptations die with them. Some use camouflage, imitation, or warning coloration to survive. Others work with their neighbors in ways that benefit both species.

A tiger will usually stay on the ground to stalk and ambush its prey. Its coat has vertical black and dull orange stripes that blend in with the tree trunks and tall shrubs of the forest floor.

Camouflage is any disguise that helps a creature blend with its background. Many animals use their color, shape, and behavior to hide in the rain forest. This can give them an edge over the animals they hunt and the animals that hunt them.

The large cats that live in the rain forest rely on the patterns of their fur to hide from their prey. A jaguar's bright orange coat with black spots may seem very bold and easy to see. In the rain forest, though, the pattern is a perfect disguise. The colors of its coat blend in with the dappled light that filters down through the leaves of the rain forest canopy.

The South American potoo (po-TOO) is a nocturnal bird that hunts insects by night and rests in trees during the day. Unlike some rain forest birds, the potoo is not very beautiful. It is a dull, brownish color. The potoo rests upright on the branch of a tree, and it blends in with the bark of the tree so well that it seems to vanish.

In a world of hunters and prey, staying unseen can mean staying alive.

A jaguar spends much of its time in the trees. The big cat will wait without moving for a deer or tapir to come near.

The grass-green vine snake spends all of its time in the trees. The snake is several feet long but only a little thicker than a pencil. Its color and shape look exactly like a young vine. Scientists call this form of camouflage *mimicry*. The snake will even sway gently in the breeze to mimic the movement of a vine in a soft wind!

The grass-green vine snake simply waits quietly in a tree for its prey—young birds, frogs, and insects—to come near. At the same time, the snake remains hidden from predators.

30

Millions of insects live in the rain forests worldwide, and they are probably the most hunted rain forest dwellers. Many species have evolved clever adaptations to help them hide from birds, reptiles, mammals, and other insects. Insects are masters of disguise and imitation. In the rain forest, some insect species mimic leaves, flowers, twigs, bark, or leaf litter. If they do not move, their enemies have a very difficult time seeing them.

The eyed silkmoth has two large markings on its wings that look like the huge round eyes of a large rain forest predator. The sight of the eyes may make a hunter pause long enough for the moth to escape.

Thornbugs look like the thick, spiny thorns of many rain forest trees that other animals have learned to stay away from.

Katydids and some mantids look exactly like the leaves in which they hide. They have flat, green wings that are the exact shape and color of young leaves. Their wings even have thin veins that look just like the veins in a leaf!

Other species of leaf insect are also light green, and they look like young, living leaves. Some even have blotches that look like chew marks, as if they were leaves that had been munched on. All of these leaf insects make their disguises more effective by swinging gently from side to side. They look like leaves swaying in the breeze!

Leaf mimicry works very well. There are four moths sitting atop these leaves.

31

The heliconid butterfly (above left) is poisonous. The mechanitis butterfly (above) is not, but predators can't tell the difference.

Camouflage is an excellent tool, but some animals use just the opposite strategy. Instead of trying to blend in with their surroundings, they stand out and call attention to themselves. They avoid being eaten by having bright colors that make them easy to see and identify. These bright colors say loudly, "Don't eat me! I taste bad!" or "Stay away! I am poisonous!"

The Costa Rican caterpillar is bright yellow and green and has clumps of stinging hairs. Predators that try to eat the caterpillar get a painful sting. The next time they are out hunting, the predators remember the bright yellow and green and stay away!

In the rain forests of South America, heliconid (hee-li-KAHN-id) butterflies are black, yellow, and orange. They are also poisonous! Birds and other predators have learned that these butterflies are dangerous to eat, and they stay away from any butterfly that is black, yellow, and orange. Some harmless butterflies also have this color pattern and are protected by their resemblance to their poisonous relatives.

Milesia vespoides is another interesting mimic. This harmless fly has evolved to look exactly like a species of poisonous wasp, *Vespa cincta*. Birds that have learned to avoid the stinging wasp will stay far away from the fly as well.

The bright yellow and green colors are a warning to stay away.

This harmless rain forest fly looks exactly like a wasp, so it gets left alone by predators.

Plants also have adaptations that enable them to survive in the rain forest. Pitcher plants are epiphytes that grow on other trees but do not take nourishment from them. The pitcher plant has several containers at the end of long, thin stalks or tendrils that hang below the plant. These containers look like water pitchers, and they catch the falling rain. Insects are attracted to the pitchers because they contain sweet-smelling nectar. Once inside the lip of the pitcher, though, an insect is doomed. The inside has a waxy surface, and the insect slips to the bottom of the pitcher where the plant digests it.

Bromeliads are common plants in the rain forest. They are epiphytes, too. Some bromeliads collect water and plant debris that fall into a well in the center of the plant. The bromeliad draws food and water from these little pools. The pools actually become tiny habitats all of their own. Some species spend their entire lives inside a bromeliad pool. Others come just to visit.

Insects are common visitors to the bromeliad. Mosquitoes and giant dragonflies lay their eggs there. The dragonfly larvae feed on mosquito larvae and other small insects. Scorpions, crabs, and carnivorous beetles arrive to snatch up the resident insects. Sometimes a mammal, like the small mouse opossum, will stop by for a meal.

The pitcher plant gets its nourishment by catching insects— it is a carnivorous plant!

The bright red leaves of many bromeliad species attract hummingbirds, too.

Poison arrow frogs leave their tadpoles in bromeliads. The tadpoles stay there until they become adults.

33

Some resident ants will even damage neighboring plants to keep them from crowding their host plant.

The yellow bumps on this plant are food grown for the ants that live inside.

Cauliflory is very helpful to pollinators looking for flowers in the dim understory.

Some plants have learned to work together with rain forest creatures in order to survive. Several species provide homes for whole colonies of ants. The ants get shelter and sometimes even food from the plants. In return, the ants provide protection. The ants go on the attack if any insects or other animals try to eat the leaves of the plant. They swarm over the intruder, biting it until it gives up and goes away. Plants like these grow in the rain forests in Southeast Asia, Africa, and South America. Many of them have hollow chambers especially for the ants to live in. One epiphyte even depends on its ants for food. The ants bring fallen leaves into the chamber for themselves, and the plant takes some nutrients from the leaves as they decay inside it.

An important challenge for rain forest plants is reproduction. To reproduce, many species must transfer their pollen to a plant of the same species. Many of them have come to rely on birds, bats, and insects to spread their pollen.

Some plants grow flowers on their trunks and lower branches. This is called *cauliflory* (KAHL-i-flor-ee). Cauliflory makes it more likely a plant will be pollinated. The cocoa tree has small white flowers growing on its trunk. Insects can better see the cocoa tree's flowers there than if they grew among leaves and branches.

Plants that depend on birds for pollination usually produce large, showy flowers that are often red or orange. Bird-pollinated plants often have little or no smell. Many species of birds have a better sense of sight than smell, and they are attracted to red and orange.

There are many species of hummingbirds in the rain forest, and all are important pollinators. As they hover against the flower, they pick up pollen. When they feed at the next flower, they leave some of the pollen behind.

Plants that need insects for pollination usually produce yellow or blue flowers that have a strong scent. Some flowers smell very sweet and others smell terrible! Some plants rely on flies for pollination, and their flowers produce very bad smells. The *Aristolochia grandiflora* smells like rotting meat or animal droppings. Flies are attracted to this odor!

Euglossine bees are the only pollinators of certain species of orchids and other plants in the Amazonian rain forest. The male bee visits orchid flowers to collect fragrance from the petals. The perfumed bee will fly from flower to flower, picking up their scent. Groups of sweet-smelling males gather together, and their combined scent is strong enough to attract female bees. The orchids have helped the bees find mates, and the bees have helped the orchids reproduce.

The pollen of many plants is located deep inside the flower. Hummingbirds use their long thin bills and tongues to reach into the flowers and sip the sweet nectar.

The color of a flower is one thing that attracts pollinating animals— red and orange for birds, blue and yellow for insects.

Euglossine bee

35

WE DESTROY RAIN FORESTS

at a frightening rate. More than 50 acres vanish every minute! Wild-life disappears with every acre. We  may be causing the extinction of species that we don't even know exist.

The situation is serious but there is hope. If we all pitch in and learn ways to protect rain forests, perhaps they will be around for a long, long time.

People need rain forests no matter where they live. Many of the foods, medicines, and household items we depend on come from the rain forest. Rain forest plants have an important effect on the worldwide climate, too. Perhaps more important than what rain forests offer us now is what they may have in store for our future.

Bananas are familiar rain forest fruits.

The rosy periwinkle has saved many lives. An anti-cancer drug can be made from this rain forest flower.

For thousands of years, people have relied on rain forest plants for making everything from rope and cloth to ships and bridges.

The oils, saps, gums, resins, and other juices of certain rain forest plants provide things we use every day.

Rain forests supply us with many foods and products we use every day. Here are just a few common rain forest foods—allspice, avocados, bananas, black pepper, Brazil nuts, cashews, chocolate, cinnamon, coconuts, coffee, ginger, grapefruits, lemons, oranges, tapioca, tea, and vanilla. Wild relatives of rice, wheat, and corn also grow in the rain forest. These food crops supply most of the world's diet. Perhaps one of the most important plant products is rubber. Chewing gum, perfumes, cosmetics, scented soaps, and cooking oils often contain ingredients from rain forest plants.

Rain forest trees such as teak, mahogany, and ebony provide some of the most beautiful and durable wood in the world. Fibers from the inner layers of tropical vines end up in clothing and textiles, twine and rope, backing for carpet and linoleum, and insulation.

We also use the rain forest like a medicine cabinet. Plants that grow only in the rain forest give us many important drugs, and we have studied only a few of them for their possible uses.

Some scientists believe that a plant that holds a cure for cancer or AIDS could be growing somewhere in a rain forest, waiting for us to find it. Or the very last of its species could be uprooted and destroyed by a bulldozer any minute.

38

Rain forests are the permanent home of hundreds of groups of indigenous, or native, people. Many of these groups have lived in the rain forest for thousands of years. They know the rain forest very well and have unlocked many of its secrets.

We can learn much from these people about the rain forest. They can teach us things it would take scientists years to discover. They can also serve as an example of the way to use the rain forest—with care and respect. As we clear rain forest lands, we force these people from their homes. In destroying the rain forest, we may be destroying their way of life.

Rain forests are important to the general health of Earth. The millions of plants living in the world's rain forests may help control weather patterns all over the world.

Rain forest plants also affect the gases in our atmosphere. All plants take carbon dioxide from the air and release oxygen into the air. The rain forest contains so many plants that they have a big effect on the atmosphere worldwide. The balance of gases in our atmosphere is one of the things that makes life on Earth possible. Rain forests have been helping to keep this balance for millions of years. Some of the oxygen you're breathing right now may have come from deep in the rain forests of Africa or South America.

South American Indians have used these two plants as medicine for centuries.

Rain forests grow only in a few places, but they are extremely important to all people.

Like many other inhabitants of the African rain forest, the native tribes are losing their homes.

Loggers often destroy all the plants in a patch of rain forest to get at the few trees that they want.

Our rain forests are in trouble. They are disappearing at the rate of more than 50 acres per minute. We have already destroyed 40 percent of the world's rain forests. Rain forests have been around for millions of years, but most of their destruction has happened in just the last 50 years! When we destroy a single acre of rain forest, we could destroy forever the treasures that it holds.

Slash-and-burn farming has destroyed millions of acres of rain forest.

Rain forests are being destroyed for many reasons. Poverty and rising populations in rain forest regions play a big role. Governments in some tropical countries see the rain forests as one of their only natural resources. Income from exploiting the rain forest is a **$** way for them to improve living conditions in their countries quickly. In modern countries around the world, rain forest products are in demand more and more. This encourages people to continue stripping the rain forests bare. The danger faced by the rain forests comes from the cultures, economies, and governments of many countries. It will be a difficult problem to solve.

The biggest threat to the rain forest is slash-and-burn agriculture. This is a common method of farming in the tropics. Slash-and-burn farmers clear small patches of rain forest by cutting down the trees and plants, carrying away the useful ones, and burning the rest. The farmers can then plant their crops.

It doesn't take much to turn a rain forest full of life into an empty wasteland.

Many native rain forest people have been practicing slash-and-burn agriculture for thousands of years. The native groups have always been small, though. Today, thousands and thousands of people leave over-crowded cities every year to escape poverty. Many become slash-and-burn farmers. Up to 20 million acres of forest are cleared each year in the tropics for agriculture. The rain forest soil is so thin that crops can only be grown on the cleared land for a few years. When farmers' lands become infertile, they move deeper into the forest. The area they leave behind is like a wasteland—few plants can grow there.

Logging also threatens the rain forest. About 10 million acres of rain forest are lost to logging every year. Much of the wood is cut by local people for firewood or charcoal, and they also use it for building houses, fences, and other things. Commercial logging operations also damage the rain forest. Sometimes all of the plants and trees in an entire area are cut down just to take a few of the most valuable hardwood trees.

Rain forests protect the land on which they grow. They recycle nutrients and waste. They keep soil erosion under control. They also act as a buffer to the land when earthquakes, tropical storms, or landslides strike. When rain forests are cut down, the land is left vulnerable.

Madagascar is a small island off the coast of Africa. Many of its rain forest inhabitants are found nowhere else in the world. This rice farm used to be part of Madagascar's rain forest. The aye-ayes, lizards, insects, ferns, and flowers that once lived here are all gone. The rice farm will be gone soon, too, once the soil loses all of its nutrients.

In Costa Rica, a coffee plantation that will survive only a few years has taken the place of a rain forest that had survived for thousands and thousands of years.

Large tracts of rain forest are also cleared to raise cattle. Millions of acres of rain forest, mostly in Central and South America, are turned into pastures for grazing. But the thin rain forest soil can only support cattle for a few years.

41

WE DESTROY RAIN FORESTS

If we all work together and change our lives in a few simple ways, we *can* make a difference!

Recycling paper, plastic, glass, and other reusable materials can help the rain forest. If we learn to waste less, we won't have to take so much from our wilderness areas.

The loss of the world's rain forests is a serious problem, but the situation is not hopeless. You don't need to be a scientist to help protect the rain forest. All you need to do is care about the rain forest and learn some simple things that will help you avoid being part of the problem.

The first step toward solving any problem is to learn as much as you can about it. Become better informed about the rain forest by reading books and magazines. Share what you have learned with your friends and family. If you help people learn about rain forests, they may want to help protect them.

Make your opinion known. You may be too young to vote, but you can still make your voice heard. Suggest to your teacher that your class write letters about the rain forest to your congressional representatives, to the president, or to the editor of your local newspaper.

President of the United States
1600 Pennsylvania Avenue
Washington, D.C. 20500

Think globally! Our actions at home *do* affect what happens in other countries and in the rain forest. Our society is a very wasteful one, and this contributes to the world's economic problems. We can all learn to conserve energy and resources. Many natural resources come directly from the rain forest. Look at ways you, your friends, and your family can save energy at home and at school.

42

Encourage your parents to be careful about what they buy. And you be careful, too! Avoid pets, plants, and products that were imported illegally from the rain forest. A parrot that was bred in captivity or a tropical plant that was grown in a greenhouse are much better choices than their wild relatives.

Look for items that benefit the rain forest. Some companies sell products such as ice cream, candy, cereal, and cosmetics that use ingredients found only in the rain forest. Sometimes the companies donate some of the profits from these products to rain forest conservation programs. Buying these products actually helps rain forests.

Join a conservation organization. There are many excellent organizations that are working to save the world's rain forests. Find out what these groups are doing to help rain forests and support their efforts.

Check out what your local zoo, aquarium, botanical garden, or science center is doing to help protect rain forests. Many of these organizations work to save endangered rain forest species. Others raise money to support rain forest conservation. Volunteer to help these organizations with their efforts. Be one of the people who make a difference.

Caiman

Jaguar

Gorilla

When we save the rain forest, we save the creatures that live there.

These children from Belize know that people of all ages and from all countries must work together to save the rain forest.

43

GLOSSARY

Adaptations (ad-ap-TAY-shuns): Changes in a plant or animal that happen over many generations and help it to survive.

Archipelago (ar-kuh-PEL-uh-go): A group of islands and other land masses scattered across a large area of water.

Camouflage (KAM-uh-flahj): Colors, shapes, and patterns that help an animal hide in nature. Many species use camouflage to get an advantage over their predators or their prey.

Canopy (KAN-uh-pee): The area of a rain forest below the emergent layer and above the understory. The canopy is usually between 65 and 100 feet above the ground.

Cauliflory (KAW-li-flor-ee): The adaptation of flowers growing directly on the trunk or lower branches of a plant. This makes it more likely that pollinating insects will find the flowers.

Decomposer (dee-cuhm-PO-zur): Any creature that breaks down dead plant or animal matter and returns nutrients to the soil. Mold, lichen, and some insects are decomposers.

Emergent layer (EE-mur-juhnt LAY-ur): The area of a rain forest above the canopy. The emergent layer is usually between 100 and 250 feet above the ground.

Environment (in-VY-ruhn-muhnt): All the things found in an area—air, land, water, weather, plants, and animals—and the way they act together and affect each other.

Endangered species (in-DAYN-jurd SPEE-shees): A kind of plant or animal that is threatened with extinction. Orangutans, clouded leopards, and mountain gorillas are a few of the endangered rain forest species.

Epiphyte (E-puh-fyt): A plant that grows on another plant and gets its water and food from the rain and air. Epiphytes are very common in rain forests.

Extinct (ik-STEENKT): No longer existing. If every member of a species has died, the species is extinct.

Forest floor (FOR-ist flor): The area of a rain forest below the understory. The forest floor includes the area a few feet above the ground.

Habitat: (HAB-uh-tat): The place that a plant or animal lives; the special kind of environment a plant or animal needs to survive.

Invertebrate (in-VURT-uh-bruht): Any animal that does not have a backbone. Insects, worms, and spiders are examples of invertebrates.

Mimicry: (MIM-i-kree): A type of camouflage that makes a plant or animal look like another plant or animal. Some species use mimicry in order to hide. Other species use mimicry to make themselves appear dangerous so that they are left alone.

Nocturnal (nahk-TURN-uhl): Sleeping during the day and being active at night. Some animals are nocturnal in order to avoid predators.

Pollination: (pahl-i-NAH-shun): The transfer of pollen from one plant to another in order to fertilize seeds. Plants rely on wind, insects, birds, and bats for pollination.

Predator (PRED-uh-tur): Any animal that hunts, kills, and eats other animals. Leopards, bird-eating spiders, and harpy eagles are examples of rain forest predators.

Prehensile (pree-HEN-suhl): Designed to grab or hold on to things. Many rain forest animals have prehensile tails that help them to climb through the trees.

Species (SPEE-shees): A group of closely related living things that can breed with one another.

Temperate (TEM-puh-ruht): Having a mild climate that usually includes four yearly seasons of different temperatures.

Tropical: (TRAHP-i-kuhl): Having a warm climate that usually includes two yearly seasons marked by different amounts of rainfall.

Understory (UHN-der-stor-ee): The area of a rain forest below the canopy and above the forest floor. The understory is usually between five and 15 feet above the ground.

Vertebrate (VURT-uh-bruht): Any animal that has a backbone. Reptiles, birds, and mammals are examples of vertebrates.